Introduction

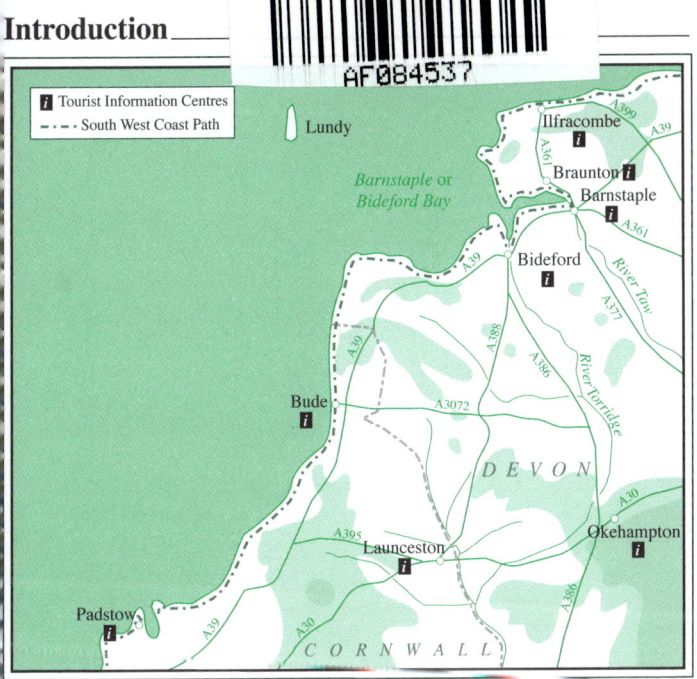

The South West Coast Path (SWCP), the longest waymarked trail in Britain, runs 630 miles/1014kms around the south west corner of England; starting at Minehead in Somerset then continuing around the coasts of Devon and Cornwall before ending at Poole in Dorset. Over its length the path passes through a great range of landscapes and provides superb walking.

Some walkers may choose to attempt the whole route – a tough undertaking, but one which is made easier by the number of towns and villages providing regular accommodation and supplies along the way. This series of guides, however, provides a different approach, suggesting a number of shorter walks – usually circuits – which can be found on a given stretch of the path. The walks included are usually relatively short, but all of them can be extended simply by continuing further along the SWCP.

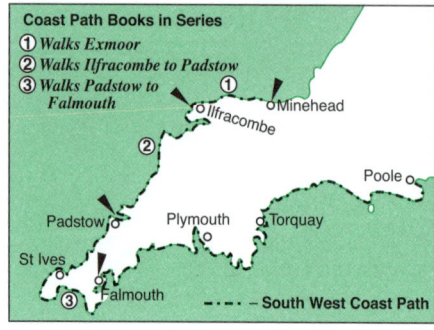

The area covered in this guide is between the handsome harbour towns of Ilfracombe in Devon and Padstow in Cornwall. The distance between them is around 58 miles/93kms as the crow flies, through the coast itself is obviously a lot longer. The geology in this section is a mixture of Devonian slates and sandstones (Ilfracombe to Barnstaple and Boscastle to Padstow) and Carboniferous sandstones and shales (Barnstaple to Boscastle), and provides some dramatic cliff scenery – notably the soft sandstone cliffs south of Bude *(Walk 14)*, the dramatic Hartland Point *(9)* and the zig-zag cliffs at Millook *(15)*.

These cliffs are one of the great attractions of the SWCP, but also its greatest danger. Please take great care when walking near the cliff tops – particularly in windy conditions – and be aware of the danger of rock falls. Sections of the path can be washed away and you must follow any directions shown on the ground. For advance warning of any problems, it is worth checking on **www.southwest coastpath.com** – a useful source of information on all aspects of the route.

It is not all cliffs, of course. This is one of the best stretches of the coast for surfing, and there are wide sand beaches at Woolacombe *(3)*, Croyde Bay *(4)*, Summerleaze *(12)*, Rock *(24)* and many other places. Some of these beaches are backed by cliffs; others – as at Woolacombe and Rock – by large areas of sand dunes.

Elsewhere there are two significant estuaries on the coast: the Taw/Torridge estuary, heading inland to Barnstaple and Bideford, and the Camel estuary, leading past Padstow up to Wadebridge. The former provides an atypical walk in this book – the dyke-top path past the bird-rich mudflats around Horsey Island down to the dunes and beaches by the estuary *(7)*.

In addition, there is one canal. The Carboniferous sandstone sands around Bude are a natural fertiliser and the Bude Canal was built to carry the sand to inland farms. What remains of the canal is now only used by pleasure craft, but the tow path provides pleasant inland walking *(13,14)*.

The larger towns along the coast – Ilfracombe, Barnstaple, Bideford, Bude, Wadebridge and Padstow – are all good service centres. Padstow is the biggest tourist centre, with its pretty harbour and mass of restaurants (for a walk from Padstow itself, *see* companion volume *Walks Padstow to Falmouth*). Ilfracombe has the most dramatic position: the old town clustered around the head of a narrow harbour with the St Nicholas Chapel – Britain's oldest working lighthouse – to one side *(2)*.

Elsewhere there are numerous smaller towns and villages, many of them highly picturesque. Perhaps the pick of these is Clovelly *(5,6)*, the car-free, private village on the Devon coast, with its precipitous cobbled street leading down to a little harbour and the steep wooded slopes to east and west.

Clovelly (see *Walks 5 & 6*)

Further south, in Cornwall, are the little villages of Crackington Haven *(16,17)* and Boscastle *(18)* in their narrow valleys – the latter particularly famous these days for the violent flash flood in 2004, when 50 cars were washed into the harbour. Still further south is Port Isaac; a beautiful little harbour town with a fishing fleet and fish market, much used as a backdrop in film and television *(22,23)*.

There are few large structures on the coast, and only one significant castle – Tintagel, the ruins of which sit on a rocky headland *(19,20)*. The ruins are medieval, but the reputation is more associated with they mythical figure of King Arthur. In the 12th century Geoffrey of Monmouth stated that Arthur had been conceived at Tintagel and the castle has been a centre of the cult ever since. Whether or not there is any truth in the story, the site is spectacular and the coastal paths to north and south equally fine.

Tintagel Castle (see Walks 19 & 20)

There is a spectacularly-sited church nearby – St Materiana's, dating from the 11th/12th centuries – and churches are another feature of the coast. There is a beautifully positioned church at St Gennys, near Crackington Haven *(16)*, and another at Morwenstow *(11)*, both of which date, in part, from Norman times. Between 1834 and 1875 the vicar at the latter was Robert Stephen Hawker, an antiquarian and poet best remembered these days as the author of *The Song of the Western Men* – the unofficial Cornish anthem, sometimes called *Trelawny*. His driftwood hut on the cliff edge can still be seen near the church *(11)*. (Another splendidly-sited writers hut, belonging to the playwright Ronald Duncan, can be seen on the cliffs south of nearby Welcombe Mouth *(10)*.)

Driving in the area is simple enough – as long as you stick to the main roads! As soon as you venture on to the minor roads – as you will need to, to reach many of these walks – things become more complicated. Leave plenty of time for journeys, work out your routes in advance and don't rush on the single-track roads. The area is so beautiful that the journeys to and from the walks are part of the pleasure of the day.

St Materiana's Church (see Walk 20)

1 Morte Point _____ B

A short stretch of public road then a clear path around the low point. The walk starts and ends at a pleasant village with an inn. Length: **3 miles/5km**; *Height Climbed:* **330ft/100m**.

O.S. Sheet 139

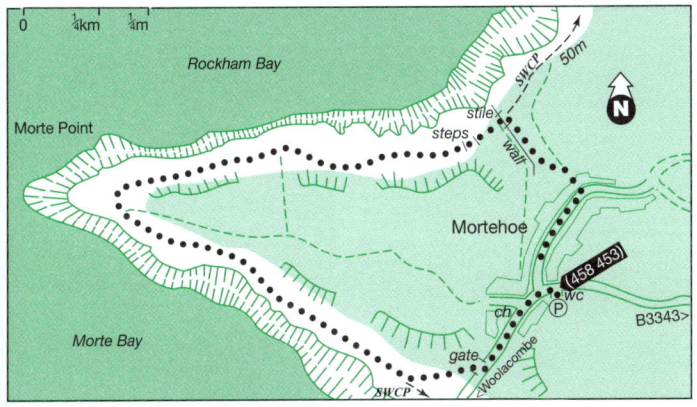

To reach the village of Mortehoe, drive 2 miles south from the centre of Ilfracombe on the A361 then turn right on the B3343. After about 2 miles turn right onto the minor road to Mortehoe.

Park in the car park, walk back out of the entrance and turn left. At the junction in the centre of the village keep left again (ie, with the church to your right). You quickly leave the village. After the last house to your right, continue downhill until you see a gate to the right of the road and a sign for a footpath. Go through this gate and follow a grassy path downhill until you are behind the shore.

Turn right along a clear path, with a low cliff down to your left, and follow it out to Morte Point. Beyond the point you get a view of the lighthouse on Bull Point and the path doubles back along the north side of the headland.

You pass signs pointing right for Mortehoe. These are possible shortcuts, but for this route continue until the path climbs steeply, on steps, to the top of a ridge. Beyond this there is a deep grassy gully with a wall running up the bottom of it.

Follow the path down to the wall and cross a stile. Beyond this there is a sign for Mortehoe pointing right, up a grassy path. Follow this up to join a clearer path and turn right (Mortehoe). The path goes through a gate then joins the road in the village between houses. Turn right to return to the start.

2 Ilfracombe _____ C

A short walk, steep in places, along a rocky shore and round a wooded hill. It is quite easy to get lost amongst the paths on the hill, but difficult to go too far wrong. The paths are generally good and the views excellent. Length: **2½ miles/4km**; *Height Climbed:* **330ft/100m**.

O.S. Sheet 139

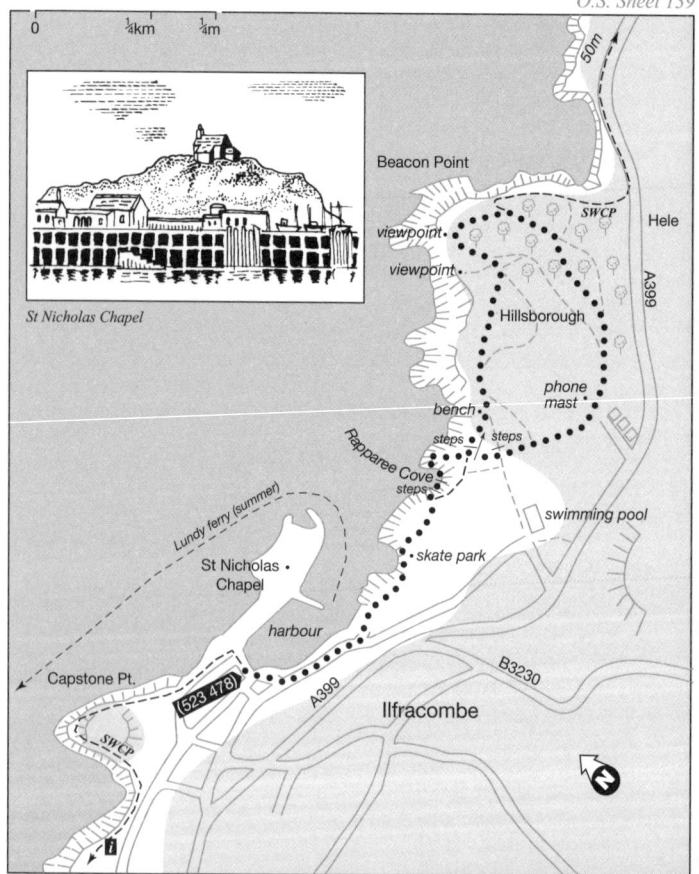

St Nicholas Chapel

Ilfracombe is a handsome town on a very picturesque site. Its most attractive feature is its harbour, which is dominated by the St Nicholas Chapel on a small hill to the north of the entrance – the oldest building in the town and reputedly the oldest working lighthouse in Britain. The town was built around this natural harbour, which provided a haven for fishermen and traders. Nowadays it is one of the two start points (the other is Bideford) for the passenger ferry to the island of Lundy.

This walk leads up the hill on the Hillsborough promontory – directly to the east of the town – which provides the best view of the harbour.

Find your way down to the harbour and start walking down its right-hand side, with the chapel visible across the harbour to your left. When the road you are on swings right, away from the water, watch for a path dropping down to the left.

You quickly pass a sign for the Coast Path and find yourself on a tarmac path behind a rocky inlet, with a skate park to your right and the outer harbour to your left. At the next inlet (Rapparee Cove) steps lead down to the head of the bay then back up the other side to reach a four-way junction with five wooden-fronted steps climbing to your left. Go left here. (**NB:** At high tide the path around Rapparee Cove may not be possible, in which case you should take the shortcut shown on the map.)

You reach a junction with a clearer path, by a bench. Go left, climbing. Ignore two paths heading off to the right (there is a mass of paths on the hill, but even if you go wrong you can't get too lost) and climb to the highest point, with a view into the next bay. A path heads off to the left (viewpoint); stick to the Coast Path.

You now descend through woodland to a junction with a path heading back-right. Keep straight on (Coast Path). A viewpoint is visible ahead, with railings. Enjoy the view then double back down the slope.

The path zig-zags down the slope to join a clear path going downhill to the left and uphill to the right. The Coast Path goes left, leading to Hele, but for this walk go right, uphill.

The path quickly forks. Keep right, contouring across the slope. Continue across the slope, ignoring paths to right and left, until you pass a phone mast to the right of the path. At the same point a road comes in from the left, with houses along one side of it. Ignore this and continue across the slope.

You pass a four-way junction with steps to your right. Keep straight on to the next four-way junction – the one you were at before. Keep straight on to return by Rapparee Cove or go left to avoid it, then retrace your steps to the start.

If you are looking for another short walk in the town, walk west from the harbour for a short distance to join the network of paths on Capstone Point. There is a picturesque coast path and a climb to an excellent viewpoint on the summit.

3 Woolacombe   C

A circuit starting over a low hill, giving good views, then returning through dunes behind a wide, sandy beach. Length: **3 miles/5km***; Height Climbed:* **490ft/150m***.*

O.S. Sheet 139

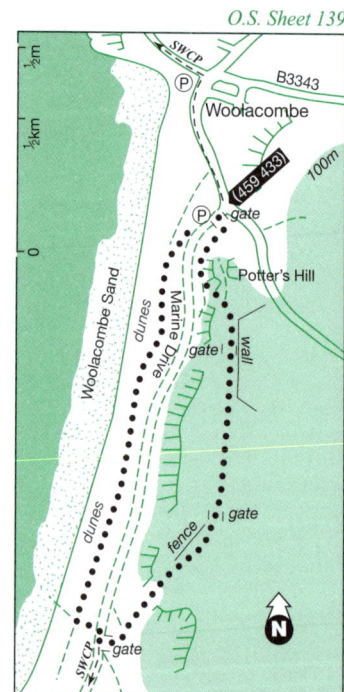

To reach the resort village of Woolacombe follow the instructions for Walk 1, but rather than turning right on to the minor road for Mortehoe, keep straight on. Drive down to the front of the village and turn left (car parks). After a short distance the pay car park on Marine Drive opens up to the right. Park here, as near the entrance as possible.

Walk back out past the pay point and look for a gate to your right and a sign for Potter's Hill. The path beyond starts roughly parallel to Marine Drive (at a fork, keep left) then curves to the left, climbing, to run along with a wall to the left.

The path climbs to reach a fence crossing the way. Go through a gate and continue, still with the wall to your left. There may be grazing animals beyond this point; avoid them and please don't feed the ponies.

When the wall pulls away to the left the path keeps straight on; climbing through grass and gorse to the highest point then descending. A fence comes in from your left, ending with a gate. Go through this and continue, now with the fence running to your right.

Keep straight on at a signposted junction and you quickly reach a gate/stile, beyond which is Marine Drive. Turn right along this for a few paces then turn left at the sign for the Coast Path. Follow the rough path down into the dunes to a four-way junction. If you keep straight on at this point you can walk along the beach. To follow the Coast Path through the dunes, go right.

Continue until you are almost back at the road and turn right, back up to Marine Drive.

4 Croyde Bay & Baggy Point — B

A coast path around a low headland with a return through farmland.
Length: 3½ miles/5.6km; Height Climbed: 430ft/130m.

O.S. Sheet 139

The village of Croyde is 4 miles west of Braunton on the B3231. From the centre, follow the signs for Croyde Bay and park in the National Trust car park before the end of the road.

Continue walking along the road. When a track heads right for a farm, keep straight on along the metalled road; passing the last of the houses then going through a pedestrian gate.

Almost immediately beyond there is a signposted split. Keep left and continue to a hairpin bend just before the point. Beyond this a narrow, grassy path continues a short way, with cliffs to either side, towards the point. You must take care here, but the views from the point are good.

Return to the hairpin bend and go left, climbing to a gate. Beyond this there is a split. Go left, initially with a fence to your left. The path edges right to join a wall and follows it round the headland, giving fine views north to Woolacombe Sand.

The path passes through one pedestrian gate then, just before a second, a sign points right for the car park. Climb up to a stile beside an old concrete bunker and walk on up the side of the field beyond with a wall to your left (grazing animals).

Walk through two fields and the farm is visible to your right. At the bottom of the second field a sign points left. Cross a stile and walk along the top of a field. At the end of the field go right, still with the wall to your left.

At the bottom corner there are two gates. Go through the right-hand (pedestrian) gate and walk up the left-hand side of the grazing area beyond. When the wall heads off to the left a sign points half-left. Follow the direction indicated to the top of Middleborough Hill.

Just below the top there is a bench with a fine view of the bay. Go ahead-left from here (post) and a clear path runs down to a kissing-gate in a wall. Walk straight downhill below this, to join the road at a stile to the left of the building visible ahead.

Turn right to return to the car park.

5 The Hobby Drive /
6 Clovelly to Blackchurch Rock _____ C/B

Two coastal walks from the picturesque, car-free village of Clovelly.
5) *A lineal, woodland track leading to a viewpoint overlooking the village. Length:* **3 miles/5km** *(there and back); Height Climbed: undulating.* **6)** *A lineal route through woodland along the cliffs (take care) west of the village, returning via a church. Length:* **4 miles/6.5km***; Height Climbed: steep undulations.* (**NB:** add **410ft/125m** to the height climbed on either walk if visiting the harbour).

O.S. Sheet 126

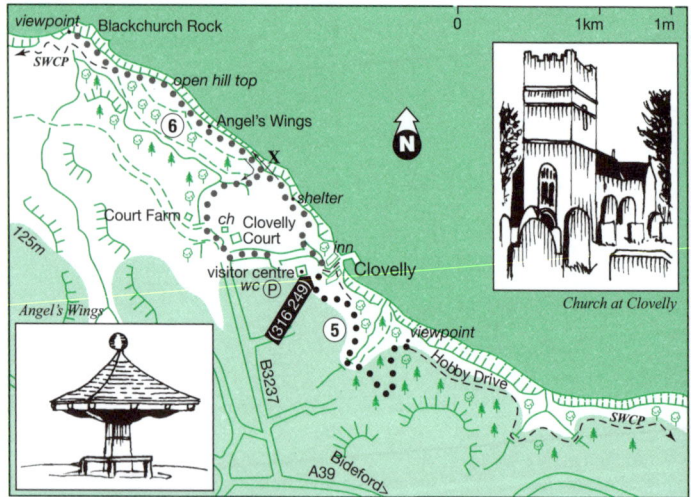

Church at Clovelly

Clovelly – 11 miles west of Bideford on the A39/B3237 – is one of the gems of the district: an unspoilt fishing village at the foot of a 410ft/125m slope. There is an old harbour and two hotels but no traffic, and goods are pulled about the steep cobbled streets on wooden sledges.

As the village is privately owned there is a fee for entrance. You park in the car park provided and approach the village through the Visitor Centre/shop. When you walk down from the Centre you quickly reach a four-way junction of roads and an information board showing the walks.

You will certainly want to visit the village. The road ahead leads straight down through the houses to the harbour. Alternatively, you can do walk

5 first and drop down to the village along the alternative return (*see* map).

Walk 5) For the shorter, easier walk, go right at the junction. You are on the Hobby Drive: a clear track which contours along the wooded slope offering fine views of the sea and coastal scenery.

After 1/2 mile/0.8km you pass a sign to your left at the start of a steep, narrow path to Clovelly. This is a possible alternative return; for now, continue along the coast.

After 1 1/2 miles/2.4km you pass some white benches to the left of the track, from where there are fine views down to the village. Return by the same route. If you are taking the alternative path to the village, turn right at the sign passed before. The path is steep in places, but junctions are marked by yellow arrows and you quickly reach the main street.

Walk 6) For the longer and more complex route, go left. You quickly pass a car park and another metalled road heads off signed for the Coast Path. Turn on to this and immediately there is a gate to the left and a sign for the Coast Path.

The path splits twice (no signs): keep right both times. Initially, the path runs through trees before leaving cover to run along the edge of the parkland around Clovelly Court (visible up to your left). Stick to the edge of the trees and you reach a kissing-gate.

Go through the gate and back into the trees. You quickly pass a stone shelter/viewpoint, with a terrific view over the sea and along the coast, then go through another gate and back into the parkland.

Follow the edge of the trees, as before, to reach the next gate. Go through this and continue through trees to reach a signposted junction (**X** on map). The track back-left (church) is your return route; for now, go ahead-right (Coast Path).

At the fork a little beyond keep right (yellow arrow) to reach a second shelter/viewpoint: the elegant 'Angel's Wings'. The path then continues along the top of the slope before joining another track. You immediately leave this to the right to continue along the top of the slope.

The path quickly reaches a gate, beyond which you climb through grass and gorse to an open hill top, from which there is a terrific view. Descend beyond to reach a gate and go back into the trees.

The path descends to a double junction. Go right at both (viewpoint) and follow a clear path along the narrow headland to an old pavilion and a superb viewpoint.

Retrace your steps to junction **X** and go right. Ignore tracks heading off first right then left and you will find yourself walking along with a stream to your right. When you reach a track crossing the stream on a stone bridge, turn left along it.

This track leads you up to the church by Clovelly Court, then on up to the public road. Turn left along the road (there is a pavement) to return to the car park.

7 Velator & Horsey Island _____B

A low-level circuit along dykes, leading down a tidal creek to an area of dunes with a sand beach beyond. Length: **5½ miles/9km**; *Height Climbed:* negligible.

O.S. Sheet 139

To reach the start of this walk, follow the signs for Barnstaple from the centre of Braunton (A361), but turn right at a roundabout (Velator Ind. Est.) At the next, keep straight on. After a short distance there is a car park directly to the left of the road, with boats in the River Caen beyond.

Immediately beyond the car park there is a bridge over the drainage ditch to your left. Cross this to reach the wall by the river and turn right, downstream.

After a short distance the toll road begins, down to your right. Continue between the road and the river until the road peels off to the right, with a grassy wall beside it. That is your return route; for now, stick to the path by the river, with small boats anchored in the channel and birds feeding on the mud.

When the Caen joins the Taw the path on the wall swings right and continues to a junction with the metalled toll road by the white Crow Beach House.

To make the lineal extension to the beach, turn left here and follow the rough road past a car park to a junction. Keep straight on, along a duckboard path through the dunes, to reach the wide sands of the beach (NB: there is a military training area nearby; keep out of the way of any troops movements.)

Retrace your steps to Crow Beach House and start along the toll road. A path quickly starts along the top of the mound to the right of the road. Follow this back to the original path.

8 Hartland Quay_____B

A dramatic section of coastal path, with steep undulations, with a return through farmland. Fine cliff scenery. Length: **4 miles/6.4km**; *Total Height Climbed:* **490ft/150m**.

O.S. Sheet 126

To reach the start of this walk, drive 10 miles west from Bideford on the A39, then turn right on the B3248 to Hartland. Drive straight through Hartland, and Stoke beyond, following the signs for Hartland Quay. There is parking at the top of the slope above the Quay, but the larger car parks are behind the hotel and shops at the foot of the slope.

For this walk you will be heading south (ie, turning left at the foot of the slope). The Coast Path can be joined from either of the lower car parks.

The first mile, along the coast, is undulating but perfectly clear: along low cliffs; behind the dramatic St Catherine's Tor; to the top of higher cliffs then steeply downhill to the little lawn, waterfall and stony beach at Speke's Mill Mouth.

Walk up the track up the valley. After a short distance a footbridge crosses the stream to the right; ignore this and continue a short way to reach a fork. Go ahead-left, on a grassy path climbing the side of the valley.

You reach a house at the end of a metalled road. Pass to the right of the house and walk on along the road. At the top of the slope there is a farm entrance to the left. Ignore this and continue along the quiet public road until you reach a four-way junction. Go left (unsuitable for motors).

You come down to the entrance to Wargery Farm. Turn left immediately before reaching the buildings on a clear track, heading directly for the church tower in Stoke.

The track descends to cross a stream then climbs the far slope, passing a house then continuing as a metalled road into Stoke. Turn left in the village. To avoid the road for the last section, go to the far corner of the churchyard to find the start of a path which runs parallel to the road, back down to Hartland Quay.

9 Hartland Point _____ B

A coastal cliff walk (care must be taken), providing a view of a lighthouse and returning through farmland. Length: **3½ miles/5.6km**; *Height Climbed:* **540ft/165m**. *Steep undulations on coast section.*

O.S. Sheet 126

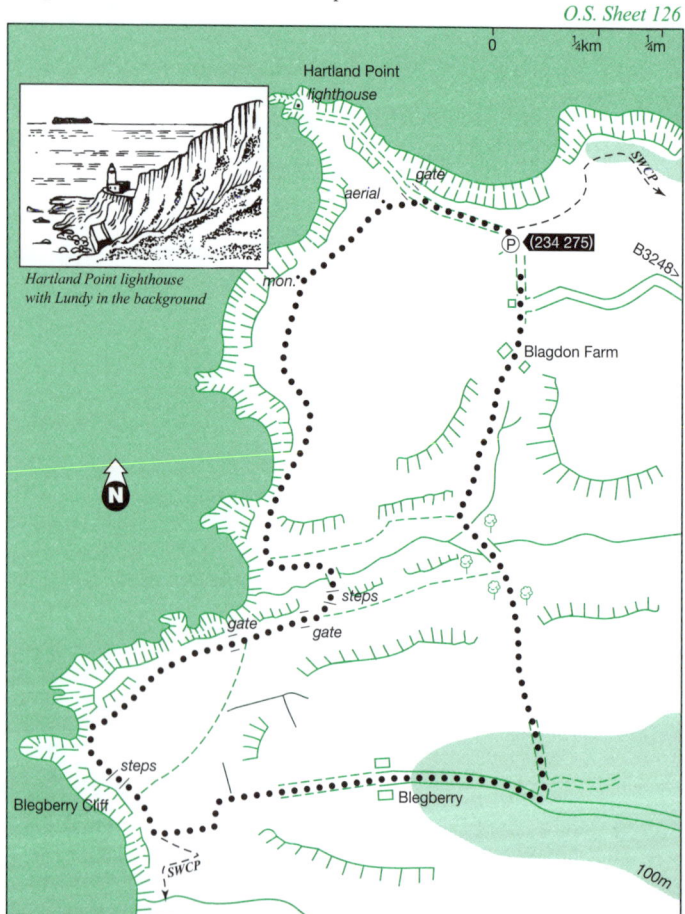

Hartland Point lighthouse with Lundy in the background

Hartland Point is the north-western tip of Devon, and technically marks the boundary between the Bristol Channel and the Atlantic Ocean. The coast here is of high, broken cliffs and there is a lighthouse (1874) on the point (visible from the walk, though it cannot be approached by walkers).

To reach the start of this walk, drive 10 miles west from Bideford on the A39, then turn right on the B3248 (for the village of Hartland). After a little over a mile there is a fork. Go right and follow the signs for Hartland Point for 5 miles to reach the pay car park at Blagdon Farm, at the end of the road.

Walk out of the end of the car park and start along the path, with the island of Lundy visible to your right. When you reach the gate for Hartland Lighthouse (private), go left (Coast Path). A cement path leads to a fence around an aerial. Go left here (arrow) on a rough path with grazing land to your left and rough grass and gorse at the top of the slope to your right.

Go through a gate and continue inside the next field. You pass a little monument to the Glenart Castle (a British hospital ship sunk in the Bristol Channel during the First World War) then, just beyond, go right (Coast Path), through a line of scrub, and continue in the same direction.

The clear path continues along the cliffs then descends towards a rocky gully. The path turns left, up the near side of the gully. When the gully ends, cross a footbridge over a stream and climb the steep steps beyond.

At the top of the slope turn right, through a gate, and continue along the edge of a field. At the end of the field there is a signposted junction. Go straight on (Coast Path), through a gate, and follow a track down the slope with views of sea rocks ahead.

Follow the path across a low area then, level with an outcrop of cliffs, a sign points left. Follow a path and a flight of steps up a steep ridge with cliffs to the right. At the junction at the top go straight on (Coast Path).

Just before the path descends again there is a sign pointing left for Blegberry. Follow this up the right-hand side of a field, with the farm buildings visible ahead. Half way up the field a sign points left, up a line of rough grass. Follow this to the top of the slope then turn right; initially along the edge of the field, then on a clear track leading to the farm.

Walk straight through the farm buildings and continue a short way along the road beyond until there is a sign for a bridleway pointing left. There are two tracks here: take the left-hand one, between hedges.

Approaching the low point of the lane, ignore a footpath heading left and continue to cross a footbridge over a little stream in the trees. Beyond that you go through a pedestrian gate and quickly reach two signposted junctions. Keep right at both (Blagdon).

Pass through a gate and follow the edge of a small, narrow field. From the next gate, the farm buildings are visible ahead.

Walks Ilfracombe to Padstow

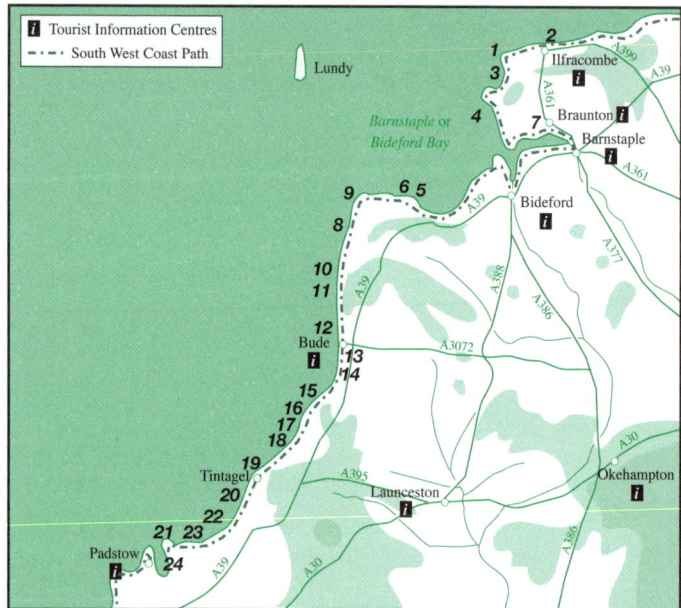

Grades

A ...... Full walking equipment required. Underfoot conditions occasionally wet or rough and some navigation may be needed.

B ...... Strong walking footwear and waterproof clothing required. Underfoot conditions generally good and navigation largely straightforward.

C ...... Comfortable walking footwear recommended.

— www.pocketwalks.com —

Published by: Hallewell Publications, The Milton, Foss, Pitlochry PH16 5NQ
Printed by: J Thomson Printers, Glasgow

While every care has been taken in the preparation of this guide, the publishers cannot accept responsibility for any loss, damage or injury resulting from its use.

Walks Ilfracombe to Padstow

walk	grade
1. Morte Point	B
2. Ilfracombe	C
3. Woolacombe	C
4. Croyde Bay & Baggy Point	B
5. The Hobby Drive	C
6. Clovelly to Blackchurch Rock	B
7. Velator & Horsey Island	B
8. Hartland Quay	B
9. Hartland Point	B
10. Welcombe Mouth	B
11. Morwenstow	B
12. Bude & Northcott Mouth	C
13. Bude & Compass Point	B
14. Bude Canal & Coast	A
15. Millook	B
16. Crackington Haven & St Gennys	B
17. Crackington Haven & Cambeak	B
18. Boscastle	B
19. Tintagel & Barras Nose	B
20. Tintagel to Trebarwith Strand	B
21. Pentire Point & The Rumps	B
22. Port Isaac	C
23. Port Isaac to Port Quin	A
24. Rock	C

10 Welcombe Mouth _____ B

A short loop with steep coastal undulations, through farmland and a wooded valley. Length: **3 miles/5km**; Height Climbed: **660ft/200m**.

O.S. Sheet 126

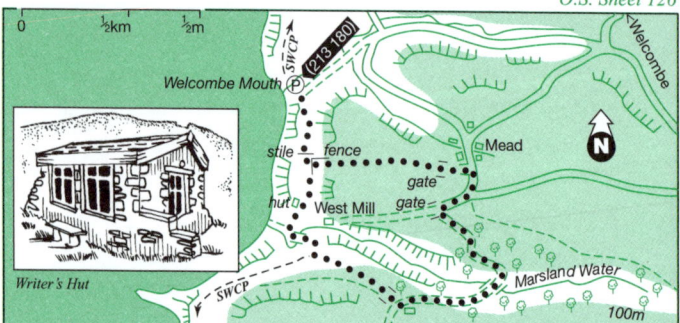

The start of this route is not easy to find. Drive 9 miles north from Bude on the A39 and turn onto the minor road for Welcombe. From the village follow the signs for Welcombe Mouth, which is on the coast at the foot of a narrow valley. The last stretch is along a rough-looking track, at the end of which there is a car park above the low cliff behind the beach.

Walk back up the entrance track and you quickly reach a sign for the Coast Path to your right. Climb steeply to a stile over a fence. Just ahead the corner of a wall is visible, with a sign pointing left.

Go left here (Mead); over a stile and up the left-hand side of two fields to reach a gate/stile. Carry straight on beyond to reach the public road.

Turn right along the road and you quickly reach another junction. Go right (Morwenstow). This road is a dead-end (for cars) and soon ends at a gate. A track goes straight on at this point, but for this walk go left, following a high-sided lane down and across the wooded slope.

While still descending, the track doubles back to reach a footbridge over Marsland Water. Cross this and follow the track up the far slope to a junction at the top of the trees.

Go right. Near the edge of the trees there is a gate, with two paths signposted beyond. Go ahead-right, down and across the slope. You descend to a three-way junction with a yellow arrow pointing left. Go straight on here: down to a footbridge over the river.

On the far side there is a split. Take the right-hand path, climbing steeply to reach the playwright Ronald Duncan's writing hut (open to walkers). Enjoy the views then continue a short distance to rejoin the original path.

11 Morwenstow — B

A circuit comprising a short stretch of cliff, two wooded valleys and a fine old church. Length: up to **3 miles/5km**; Total Height Climbed: **660ft/200m**.

O.S. Sheet 126

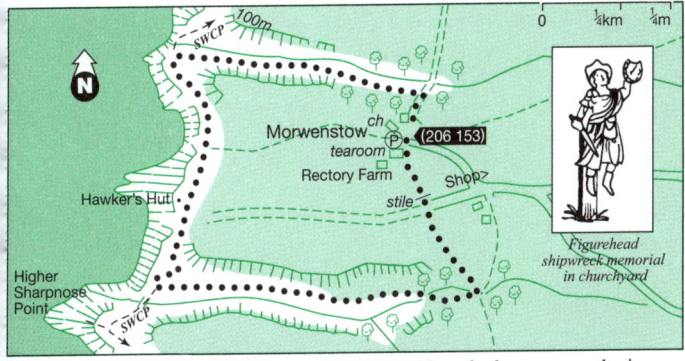

Drive 7 miles north from Bude on the A39 and turn on to the minor road to Shop. From Shop follow the signs for Morwenstow. The road is a dead-end, with the church to the right and tearooms and a car park to the left.

Walk back the way you came then turn right past the end of some farm buildings (footpath). A track leads past the buildings to a gate/stile. Walk up the left-hand side of the field beyond to reach a stile into a lane. Go straight across then down the right-hand side of the field beyond.

Go straight ahead at the far end of the field, crossing three stiles in quick succession, to join a rough path going downhill through trees.

Descend to a signposted junction by the stream in the valley and go right (Coast Path), following a clear path out of the trees and down to the coast. Near the bottom a path zig-zags up the slope to the right. That is the route for the walk, but if you don't mind heights it is worth making a brief diversion on the left-hand path: over a footbridge and on to the dramatic Higher Sharpnose Point. The views are terrific.

Retrace your steps and climb the zig-zag path. Once at the top continue through fields, watching for the path to the left to Hawker's Hut – another terrific viewpoint. When the fields end, descend into the next valley. Just before crossing the stream turn right onto a rough path (Conservation Walk).

Walk up the valley, entering a wood, until you reach a junction with a clear track. Turn back-right along this; up past the Old Vicarage and past the splendid old church.

12 Bude & Northcott Mouth /
13 Bude & Compass Point _____ C/B

Two short walks from Bude. **12)** *A simple, lineal walk past beaches and across open ground to a quiet bay. Length:* **3 miles/5km**; *Height Climbed: undulating.* **13)** *A short loop starting by the Bude Canal and returning along the coast. Length:* **2 miles/3km**; *Height Climbed:* **150ft/45m**.

O.S. Sheet 111 & 126

Bude is a pleasant resort town at a break in the cliffs where the River Neet joins the sea by a wide sand beach. This beach explains the old canal which starts at the town (*see* also Walk 14). The cliffs on this stretch of coast are sandstone, and the sand produced was carried inland on the canal to be used as fertiliser.

There are two main car parks in the town.

Walk 12) For the walk heading north, look for the car park for Summerleaze Beach, at the west end of the town to the north of the River Neet.

Walk out the back of the car park (ie, past the RNLI shop) on a metalled road. To avoid traffic, edge up the slope to your right to reach the end of a terrace. Where the road past the houses ends a metalled path continues along the coast.

Pass above the outdoor swimming pool and descend to the buildings behind Crooklets Beach. Walk along behind the beach and keep left – round the last of the houses – on the far side of the bay to reach a kissing-gate leading on to Maer Down.

Walk along the clear path behind the low cliffs until a white bungalow is visible ahead. Aim to the right of this to find a gate with a clear path beyond. Follow the path to the beach at Northcott Mouth.

Return by the same route.

Walk 13) For the walk to the south of the river, look for the car park by the Tourist Information Centre, between the River Neet and the Bude Canal. (**NB:** for a longer version of this walk, *see* Walk 14.)

Walk across the road bridge over the canal (ie, heading towards the Falcon Hotel). Cross the road (Vicarage Road) and turn left. After a short distance – just before the road begins to climb – there are signs pointing right for the Coast Path and Efford Down Stables. Turn up this metalled track.

When you reach the buildings at the end of the lane there is an opening to the right. Ignore this and keep straight on. Level with the end of the buildings the track swings right. When you reach a gate, cross a stile beside it and turn left on a clear track, heading roughly in your original direction.

The track leads to a farm gate. Go through that and continue up the left-hand side of the field beyond to reach a kissing-gate leading onto the open ground above the cliffs.

Turn right (the cliffs are crumbling in places, so stay back from the edge) and climb to a trig point. Beyond this the path descends to a gate in a wall. From this stretch there are fine views of Bude, the little tower on Compass Point and the island of Lundy beyond.

Beyond the tower the path swings right to reach the metalled path leading out to the harbour breakwater. Turn right along this and it leads to the end of the public road.

Follow the road parallel to the canal. In a short distance you can drop down to the towpath and follow it back to the start.

14 Bude Canal & Coast _____ A

A circuit starting along a canal towpath, crossing farmland then returning along the cliffs. **Length: 6 miles/10km**; **Height Climbed: 330ft/100m**.

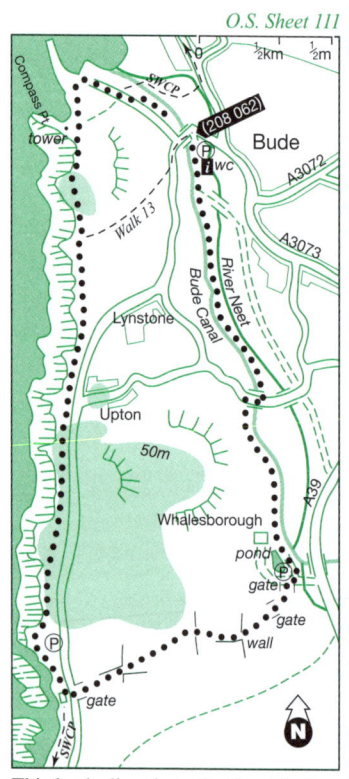

O.S. Sheet 111

Park in the car park by Bude Tourist Information Centre, between the river and the canal, then climb onto the towpath on the near side of the canal and turn left.

Continue until the first road bridge crosses the canal. At that point you cross the bridge and continue up the right-hand side.

Continue until the canal is about to run under the A39. At that point there is a split in the waterway and a signposted junction. Go straight on (Widemouth Bay), passing through a car park to join the public road.

Turn right, with a pond to your right and a cafe visible at the top of the slope ahead. After a short distance a sign points left for a footpath. Turn off here, through a gate into a field, and follow a grassy path to the top of the field (keep out of the way of grazing animals).

There is a gate at the top of the field, beyond which an unploughed strip runs across the middle of a field. That leads to a gap in a wall, beyond which you follow a track up the left-hand side of the next field.

In the next field an unploughed strip heads half-left, to the top corner of the field. Go down the right-hand side of the final field to reach a gate leading on to the public road.

Cross the road and there is a sign pointing to the right of a white house. This leads directly to the Coast Path. Turn right along this, between the cliff top and the road, and follow it for two miles/3km to the Compass Point Tower, then on into Bude by the canal towpath.

15 Millook   B

A short loop along cliff tops and up a wooded valley, passing a narrow beach. Steep undulations. Length: **3 miles/5km**; Height Climbed: **660ft/200m**.

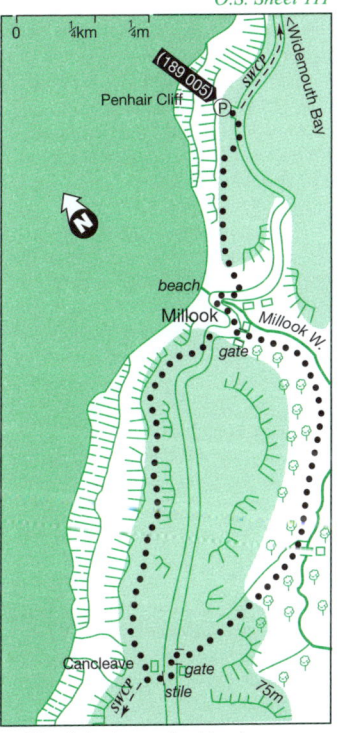

Widemouth Bay is 2 miles south of Bude by the coast road. ½ mile further south there is a junction and the coast road (Millook) becomes narrower. Follow it for a mile to reach the car park at the high point of Penhair Cliff.

Walk a short way on along the road and the Coast Path starts to the right of the road. This runs by the cliff top for a short distance then descends steeply to the hamlet of Millook behind its narrow beach.

At the bottom of the slope turn right along the road, passing the beach and starting to climb. Just before the first hairpin a sign points left for a footpath. Go through a field gate and start walking up a clear track up the side of the valley.

Go past houses and into a wood, sticking to the right of the Millook Water and ignoring bridges to your left. There is open ground to the left for a stretch before the trees start again. At that point you reach a house and a sign points right for Cancleave.

Follow a rough, clear path up the wooded slope, eventually leaving the trees at a gate and continuing with a fence and trees to your left and a grassy area to your right. Climb to a hedge, visible ahead. Cross a stile here and climb straight up the field beyond, aiming for a gate to the right of a stone building.

You join the road with a house opposite. Turn left for a few paces and there is a stile to the right and a sign for the Coast Path. This quickly leads to the cliff-top path. Turn right and follow this and the public road back to Millook.

16 Crackington Haven & St Gennys _____ B

A short, steep, undulating loop leading to superb cliff scenery and an old church. Length: 3½ miles/5.6km; Total Height Climbed: 920ft/280m.

O.S. Sheet 111

Crackington Haven is a tiny village of scattered houses at the head of a narrow beach, 9 miles north of Tintagel on the B3263 and minor roads.

Walk to the back of the car park and turn left on a metalled path. When this joins the road turn right, for a short distance. On the near side of a thatched cottage go left, at the sign for the Coast Path.

The path runs up and across the slope until it reaches a junction at the neck of narrow Pencannow Point. A short detour to the left (being careful of the cliffs) leads to a fine view. Return to the CP and continue.

The path heads inland to a gate in a fence. Immediately beyond is a signposted junction. The path ahead is your return route; for now go left (CP), by the fence. You quickly reach a deep valley. The path descends to join a fence. Go right along that until you reach a kissing-gate. Beyond that the path drops steeply to reach a footbridge over a stream with a stile just beyond. Cross this then follow the path as it zig-zags up the far slope then heads right along a narrow ridge.

Continue to the lowest point of the ridge then turn right at a signposted junction (St Gennys). The rough path descends through dense vegetation to reach a footbridge over the stream.

Climb a few steps and you are out of the vegetation and into a field. At the top of the first slope the path virtually disappears; just keep straight on to reach a gate/stile at the top of the field, marked by a yellow arrow. Beyond this you are on a metalled driveway, with a house to your right. Continue uphill, following the signs.

You reach a junction with the public road. Turn right for a short distance to reach a turning circle at the end of the road. The picturesque, partly-Norman, church is to the right of the road.

To continue the walk, look for a rough path leading uphill to the left of the road. This leads to a gate into a field.

Walk up the right-hand side of the field. At the corner, go left and keep straight on – through one more gate – to rejoin to the original path behind Pencannow Point.

17 Crackington Haven & Cambeak _____ B

A steeply undulating circuit, starting up a wooded valley and returning along the cliff tops. Some care is needed with navigation. Length: **4 miles/6.4km**; *Total Height Climbed:* **660ft/200m**.

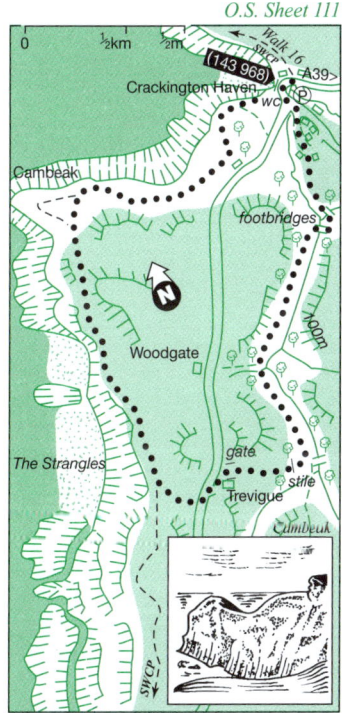

O.S. Sheet 111

Park as for Walk 16, walk out the car park entrance and turn left along the road, crossing the river. A road heads right to Trevigue. Ignore this and continue for another 40 paces, then turn right onto a driveway.

This is an access drive for houses. When it hooks back left keep straight on along a clear track (yellow arrow) then a rough path through scattered trees.

This leads to a footbridge over a stream. Cross this and keep right at the signposted junction just beyond (Sheepdip). This quickly leads to a second footbridge. Cross this and turn left on a clear path by the stream.

After ½ mile/0.8km there is another signposted junction. Keep straight on (Sheepdip) by the stream. This path soon emerges from the trees and runs along the foot of a field before reentering the trees and reaching another junction. Go right (Trevigue); climbing steeply to a stile then walking straight up the field beyond (there is no path: aim for the hedge on the horizon and avoid grazing animals).

Go through a gap at the top of the field then follow a grassy track to a gate to the right of the buildings at Trevigue. Go through this, out of the entrance to the farm and left along the public road beyond. After a short distance, as the road turns left, turn right, onto a track.

A lane between hedges (Strangles) leads down to the cliff top. Go right on a rough path. This – in a series of undulations – leads past the spectacular broken headland of Cambeak (worth exploring, but take care), then turns east to return to the start.

18 Boscastle ─────────────────────────────────── B

A short, steep circuit passing a lookout station, a fine old church and terrific coastal scenery. Length: **2½ miles/4km**; *Height Climbed:* **410ft/125m**.

O.S. Sheet 111

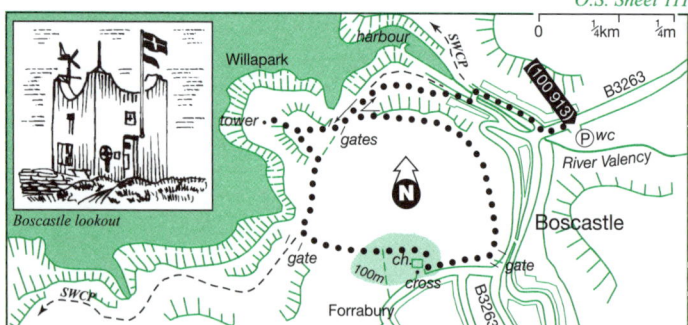

Boscastle is a small coastal village in a narrow valley, 3 miles north-east from Tintagel on the B3263. Park in the car park and walk down towards the harbour, on the right-hand side of the river. Beyond the visitor centre and shops turn left, over a bridge, at a sign for the Coast Path to Willapark.

Immediately there is a split, with the road continuing to the harbour and the Coast Path signposted ahead-left. Take the left-hand path; climbing up and across the slope with fine views down to the river. Beyond the harbour the path swings to the left and continues climbing.

Pass the sign for the Circular Path to your left and continue to a signposted junction at two gates. Go ahead-right (Willapark) and follow the path out to the square, white block of Boscastle Lookout. The views are terrific, but be careful by the cliffs.

Walk back the way you came, but go right on at a split to rejoin the Coast Path slightly further on. Turn right along this, with a wall to your right. Go past a rocky inlet to reach a junction by a gate in the corner of the field. Go left here (Forrabury), pulling away from the fence and aiming for the church tower.

Follow the grassy path to the left of the church. At the end of the churchyard there is a junction. Go right (yellow arrow). At the next corner of the churchyard a second arrow points left. Go that way, with a fence to your right, but before doing so it is worth going through the gate to your right to see the Forrabury Cross – an ancient granite monument.

At the next corner there is a kissing gate ahead of you. Ignore that and go left, following the white arrows of the Circular Path back to the Coast Path.

19 Tintagel & Barras Nose_____B

A cliff top walk (take care), passing a large headland and the entrance to the ruin of Tintagel Castle. Length: **2½ miles/4km**; *Height Climbed:* **330ft/100m**. *Possible link with Walk 20.*

O.S. Sheet 111

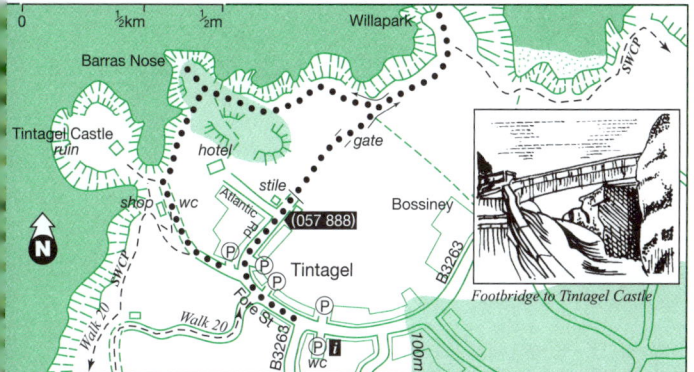

Footbridge to Tintagel Castle

Park in one of the car parks in Tintagel and walk down Fore St (ie, towards the sea), which then swings right into Atlantic Road. Follow this until it turns hard left, towards the hotel. At this point keep straight on, down a track between houses (to Coast Path).

At the end of the lane there is a farmyard to the right. Cross a stile beside a gate and walk on down the right-hand side of a field (keep out of the way of any grazing animals). At the end of the field there is a small gate, beyond which you are outside the field boundaries.

A path continues in the same direction. After a short distance there is a junction with a path heading back-left. This is the Coast Path – your return route – but for now keep on; behind a bay then out along a large, cliff-edge headland, visible ahead. Enjoy the views (while keeping away from the edges) and return to the junction.

Follow the clear path along the coast to a signposted junction at the neck of rocky Barras Nose. It is worth exploring the headland (with care) before returning to the main path and continuing towards Tintagel Castle, visible ahead.

The path leads to the shop and cafe at the bottom of the entrance road to the castle. If you wish to visit the castle, go right. To return to Tintagel, go left, up the entrance road. If you would like to link with Walk 20, watch for a flight of steps just beyond the shop on your right (Trebarwith Strand).

20 Tintagel to Trebarwith Strand B

A dramatic cliff top walk to a village and beach, returning through farmland and past an old church. Length: **4½ miles/7km**; *Height Climbed:* **660ft/200m**. *Possible link with Walk 19.*

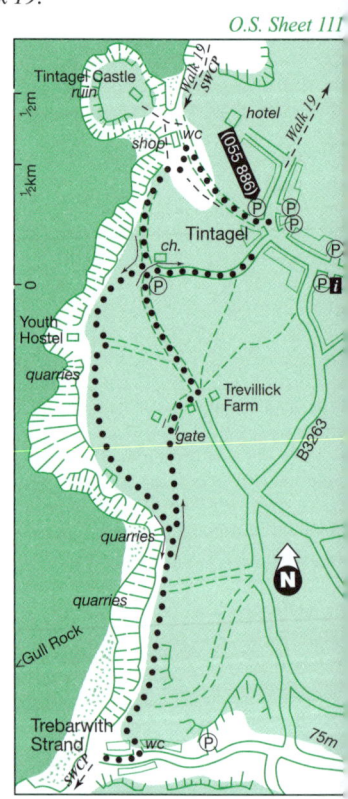

O.S. Sheet 111

Park in one of the car parks in Tintagel and walk down the access road to the castle. At the foot of the slope are a shop and a cafe. Just before the shop, to the left, there is a flight of steps (Trebarwith Strand).

Climb the slope to join another path. Turn right along this, then left at the next junction (by an entrance to the castle). Walk on a short way to cross a stile over a wall, then climb to join the end of a metalled track, with a church visible on the horizon ahead.

There is a variety of paths and tracks but no real doubt about the route; just keep on along the dramatic cliff top, past the church, a youth hostel, and some disused quarries. Once in the bay with conical Gull Rock in it, watch for a path going back-left for Trevillick. That will be your return route, but for now keep on to Trebarwith Strand, where there are shops, bars, restaurants and (if the tide is out) a beach.

Retrace your steps to the Trevillick sign and walk on to cross a stile into a field. Walk across two fields, aiming for a gate to the right of a house. Cross a stile beside the gate and you are on a track.

Follow the track to a complex junction by the road-end at Trevillick. Go left, aiming for the church. When the track splits keep straight on to reach the car park by the church.

After visiting the church – which dates from the 11th or 12th century – take the public road back into Tintagel, keeping an eye open for traffic on this narrow road.

21 Pentire Point & The Rumps — B

A path around a rocky headland, returning through farmland. Length:
4 miles/6.4km; *Height Climbed:* undulating.

O.S. Sheet 106

There is a string of villages on the east side of the River Camel, opposite Padstow. New Polzeath is the most northerly – behind the sands of Hayle Bay and with Pentire Point to the north.

Park in the car park in the village, then walk out the front of the car park and turn right. When the road swings left keep straight on, along a clear lane (sign for Port Quin). The path drops to the head of a sandy bay then climbs the far side.

After a short distance the path heads right, into a little valley. At the low point of the path there is a junction, with one path heading right for Pentire Farm. That is your return route; for now stay by the coast.

Follow the fine coastal path, with low cliffs to your left, out to rocky Pentire Point. Beyond that the path heads east and the grassy peninsula of The Rumps can be seen ahead.

The path forks as it approaches The Rumps. It is worth heading left to explore the area (with care) before returning to the main path and continuing down the far side of the larger headland.

After a short distance the walls to the right make a corner and the path forks. Go right (Pentire Farm), entering a field and walking up its left-hand side. At the far end of the field go through another gate, beyond which you turn left for a short distance to reach a further gate with a track beyond. Walk straight ahead down the track towards the farm buildings.

Pass to the right of the buildings, at the end of which a lane starts to your right. Follow this down a small valley to rejoin the original path.

22 Port Isaac / 23 Port Isaac to Port Quin _____ C/A

Shorter and longer versions of the dramatic coast walk west from the picturesque fishing harbour of Port Isaac. Steep climbs on both.
22) *A short loop around a headland and back through farmland (grazing animals). Length:* **2½ miles/4km**; *Total Height Climbed:* **330ft/100m**.
23) *A fine coast path, with steep undulations, to a hamlet behind a narrow bay. The return is through farmland (grazing animals). Length:* **5½ miles/8.8km**; *Total Height Climbed:* **755ft/230m**.

O.S. Sheet 106

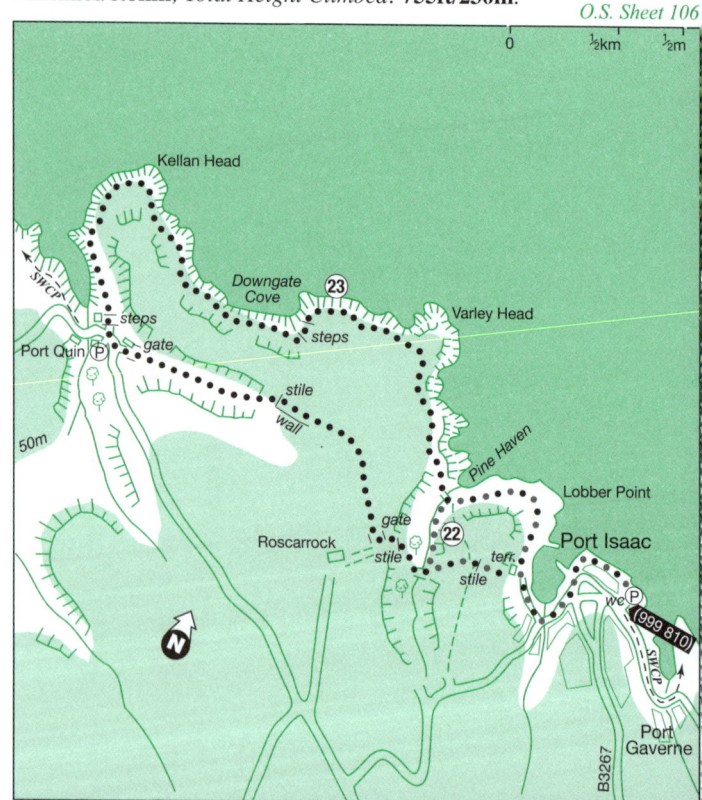

Port Isaac is a highly picturesque village and harbour – much in demand from television and film companies – about 9 miles north from Wadebridge along various roads.

Walks 22 & 23) Follow the signs for the car park, overlooking Port Gaverne. Walk down to the front of the car park and a path runs round the sea-side of the buildings before joining the road as it descends to the heart of the old village. Follow the road round the head of the bay and out the other side.

The road climbs before ending at a short terrace of houses. The path, marked by a yellow arrow, starts to the right of the entrance to the houses.

The path climbs steeply then curves through the fields on Lobber Point before descending to a signposted junction by Pine Haven.

Walk 22) Go ahead-left (footpath) and follow a rough footpath up the valley until you reach a signposted junction by a footbridge surrounded by trees. Go left (Port Isaac), climbing steeply on a clear path. (*See* last two paragraphs for end of route.)

Walk 23) Keep straight on (Port Quin); climbing steeply again.

The path cuts across the neck of Varley Head and runs along the cliffs for a short distance before descending on steps to an undulating section in the broken ground behind Downgate Cove. Beyond this it runs round Kellan Head and down to Port Quin: a tiny village with a small sand beach at the head of a narrow, rocky inlet.

The path joins the road down a flight of steps. A diversion to the right leads down to the beach, but to continue with the walk go left.

Walk a short way up the road and it begins to turn right. At this point a signposted track goes straight on (Port Isaac). Walk up to the right of a cottage to reach a gate/stile, beyond which you are at the bottom of a slope with a marshy area to your right.

Walk straight on, quickly passing through a gap in an old field boundary then continuing to a second one. Beyond this a faint path continues along the bottom of the field but you have to edge left, up and across the slope, towards two gates visible ahead.

Cross the stile by the left-hand gate and walk on with a wall to your right. This gradually bends to the right. When you draw level with Roscarrock Farm you pass through a gate and turn left (yellow arrow).

Walk downhill, down the side of the field. At the bottom corner go right for a short distance to reach a stile with a gap beside it. Go through that and you are out of the field and walking down a slope through scrub

You descend to a footbridge in trees. At the junction beyond keep straight on (Port Isaac) and climb a clear path.

Walks 22 & 23) When you climb above the trees you are in a field. Aim for the post in the middle of the field. From there, gates are visible ahead but you aim ahead-right, to a stile in a wall marked by a post.

Go down the left-hand side of the field beyond. This becomes a wooded lane and descends to the end of the road out of Port Isaac.

24 Rock

A short walk through the dunes beside the Camel Estuary. Possible access by ferry from Padstow. **Length:** *2½* **miles/4km**; *Height Climbed:* undulating.

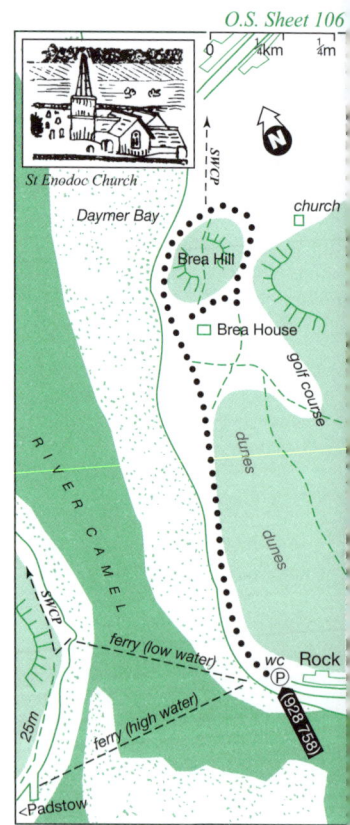

Rock is a pleasant resort village on the eastern side of the River Camel, directly opposite Padstow. It can be accessed by road from Padstow, via Wadebridge, but the more enjoyable approach is by the little passenger ferry which crosses the river from Padstow (*see* map).

However you have got there, look for the Rock Quarry car park at the far west (downstream) end of the village. The Coast Path starts from the back of the car park, with dunes to the right and the wide sands of the beach to the left – providing an obvious alternative route, if you prefer.

Whichever route you have taken, you will soon see little Brea Hill ahead, with the large white Brea House on its near side. Walk round the front of the hill and the wide sands of Daymer Bay open up in front of you, with the village of Trebetherick beyond.

Keep edging round the hill (or climb over it, if you prefer) until you return to your original path, then retrace your steps to the start.

From the back of the hill you will see little St Enodoc Church. It cannot be reached from this path (there is a stream in the way, with a golf course beyond), but it is an interesting structure. Its oldest sections date from the 12th century, and throughout the 18th century it was almost entirely buried in sand, and was only completely unearthed in 1864.